FACING
My Feelings

AuthorHouse™
1663 Liberty Drive
Bloomington, IN 47403
www.authorhouse.com
Phone: 833-262-8899

Because of the dynamic nature of the Internet, any web addresses or links contained in this book may have changed since publication and may no longer be valid. The views expressed in this work are solely those of the author and do not necessarily reflect the views of the publisher, and the publisher hereby disclaims any responsibility for them.

This book is printed on acid-free paper.

ISBN: 979-8-8230-0403-9 (sc)
ISBN: 979-8-8230-0402-2 (e)

Print information available on the last page.

Published by AuthorHouse   03/16/2023

authorHOUSE®

FACING My Feelings

JENNY QUINTANILLA

The way you feel today is okay! Sometimes you might not understand why you feel sad, mad, happy, or excited. Feelings are not right or wrong.

The first day of school, I feel nervous. I don't know my teacher. I don't know if my friends will be in my class. My parents really try to get me excited. They say," Ariana, you are smart and kind. Everyone will love you!" I get a little excited. But down deep inside, I am still nervous. Will my teacher like me? It is okay to be nervous. I will face the day with courage and be brave. I will try my best to get my jitters out. I will show my teacher that I am smart. I will get to know my classmates. They might feel the same way I do.

Sometimes I feel sad. My parents were not happy that I did not clean my room. I wanted to play instead. I take six deep breaths. I think to myself, Once I clean my room, then I can play. I know that being sad will soon go away. I start to clean my room. I look around to make sure I have put the toys in their place. It makes me feel happy that I did it. My parents are happy too.

6

I am happy when I play with my friends. I feel like I can be silly. I can pretend that I am a superhero. My friends love to pretend too. We play different games, like the floor is lava. We have fun playing together.

8

I am also happy when I am with my family. We play games together. We ride bikes around our neighborhood. We also talk at dinner time. My brother and I talk about our day at school. My brother is older. He talks about how hard his classes are.

Sometimes, I am mad. I do not like being the youngest child. My brother gets to stay up late. He gets to go out alone with his friends. My mom tells me that when I am older, I will also get to do those things. It does not make me feel better at that moment. She reminds me that I have many toys to play with. She says that his schoolwork is difficult. I guess I can wait.

There are times I get super excited. I start to get excited right before winter break, spring break, or summer vacation. Everyone needs a break also, not just me. I think about what I will do for fun. My parents sometimes plan trips for the family. Sometimes, we just do things at home. I feel relieved that I can relax and not worry about schoolwork. It is nice to always have something to look forward to.

I learned that it is okay not to be okay all the time. I am grateful to have my family, friends, and teachers that help me feel better. Each feeling is different and will change. I will face each feeling with courage. I am smart. I will be okay.

Five Ways I Can Keep Calm:

1. Take 6 deep breaths.

2. Think of a happy place and imagine I am there.

3. Stay positive. Say to myself, I am brave! I can do this! I am smart!

4. Relax my shoulders. Move my shoulders up and down.

5. Drink a cup of water.

Printed in the United States
by Baker & Taylor Publisher Services